TO
SAIL NO MORE
COLOUR EDITION - PART ONE

IAN BUXTON

Title Page: The battleship HOWE after arrival at Ward's Inverkeithing yard on 4 June 1958, outboard of the submarine depot ship MONTCLARE.

THE BRITISH SHIPBREAKING INDUSTRY POST-WAR

The period 1945-65 was a boom time for demolishing the Royal Navy's warships in British shipbreaking yards. Steel was in short supply, so recycled ship scrap helped boost output. Few of the 1200 warships (i.e. excluding small craft like LCTs, MTBs, MMSs etc) built in the Second World War were suitable for facing the threat now posed by the Soviet Union. The majority of escort vessels were of little use against a huge Soviet submarine fleet using German U-boat technology. While some ships such as cruisers and destroyers were modernised in the 1950s, the great majority were allocated to the Reserve Fleet and eventually scrapped. Some smaller vessels could be sold for conversion to civilian use e.g. tank landing craft; others were sold to friendly navies.

There were nine major British shipbreakers who could handle warships such as cruisers, six being in Scotland. But most of the sixteen or so others were limited to destroyers and below, under 400ft long and with drafts of less than 16ft. Collectively they could produce about 400,000 tons of steel scrap a year, employing directly around 3,000 workers. The steelworks could also import scrap and ships for breaking from abroad, but this required scarce foreign currency which a straitened UK economy could ill afford.

British steelmakers had set up the British Iron & Steel Corporation (Salvage) Ltd, usually known as BISCO, to procure their raw materials including iron ore, on a collective basis. So BISCO not only handled redundant British warships but bought ships from abroad, as well as British owned merchant ships. Only small local vessels like tugs could be bought directly by British breakers at that time. Contrary to what many reference books say, almost all British warships discarded between 1945 and 1962 were not 'sold' to shipbreakers. Instead they were 'handed over' to BISCO, with no money changing hands. BISCO then allocated each ship to a suitable shipbreaker as a sub-contractor and arranged delivery, often chartering commercial tugs of United Towing of Hull. The allocation was on the basis not only of the ship being able to be berthed at the breaker's yard with suitable facilities, but also their current workload and their efficiency in terms of demolition costs per ton of steel. BISCO directed each shipbreaker to which steelworks the scrap was to be despatched, but the breakers did not know the steel scrap price – deliberately kept low to help the steel industry. They did however dispose of other materials like non-ferrous metals and re-usable items like anchor cables directly to merchants and buyers. So after a warship had been demolished, BISCO added up the sales value of all materials recovered, deducted the costs of breaking including delivery of the ship, giving a resultant net value. This was then returned to the then relevant Government department, not always the Admiralty (e.g. Ministry of Power in 1958), in effect a deferred sale price. This was typically between 5 and 8% of the newbuilding cost. The Admiralty had handed over to BISCO in the four years 1954-57 481,000 standard displacement tons, half of which was made up of four battleships and four aircraft carriers. Standard displacement was the full load displacement excluding fuel and reserve feed water but including consumables like fresh water, stores and ammunition. The weight of recoverable material as noted in several captions was thus well below this displacement.

The Marine Technology Special Collection at Newcastle University's School of Marine Science & Technology holds many of the records of the British shipbreaking industry, most of which closed in the 1980s. Much of the data in the photo captions came from these records, plus notes from my own visits to the yards at the time.

THE PHOTOGRAPHS

Thomas W F Walker, who later hyphenated the F to Ferrers-Walker, had served in the RN toward the end of the war. He was keen to make his career with the Navy, but his father insisted that he join the family business, Walkers of Birmingham making small metal items like belt buckles. He eventually took over the business after his father retired, but at least it did give him the money and time to indulge his passion for warships. He was a regular visitor to the shipbreaking yards as evidenced by his photographs reproduced here. He could also afford to buy artefacts from the ships like nameplates, treadplates and gun tompions, making his house at Barnt Green a mini museum. He was well in with the shipbreakers' managers who would advise him when a warship was due, so he could fly up from Birmingham. He used both black & white and colour film in two different cameras, the latter then (1950s) very expensive both for (Kodak) film and for processing.

At that time, I was both studying naval architecture at Glasgow University and working in the Denny shipyard at Dumbarton, located close to several of the Scottish shipbreakers. The yards then worked on Saturday mornings, so I tried to visit them after a new warship arrived - with the yard's permission and at my own risk. So I first met Tom Walker (although he never used Christian name terms with me) on one of his visits to Faslane, staying at an expensive hotel in Helensburgh. He encouraged me to take a wider range of photos, but only the cheaper b&w for me until the 1960s, processing my own 120 films. I was more agile than the rather portly Tom, so could climb masts and cranes to get unusual angles looking down on the ships below. I soon learned to be wary of climbing warship mainmasts in the wake of funnel gases which corroded the rungs of their steel ladders. Tom would ask me to take his colour camera on these occasions, so some of 'his' photos are technically mine. 'Payment' would be in the form of a batch of prints, both b&w and colour. So these photos are an almost unique record of a bygone era, both the ships and the shipbreaking industry. Part 1 covers 1949 to 1962, Part 2 will cover 1962 to 1986.

Ian Buxton
Tynemouth

Literally thousands of redundant naval craft were sold by the Admiralty after the First World War. Among the many torpedo boats was No.14, 256 tons built by White of Cowes in 1908. She was sold at Devonport on 7 October 1920 for £1,257 to shipbuilders Philip & Son Ltd at Dartmouth. Stripped of valuable materials at nearby Noss, her hulk was used as a floating pontoon with a gangway to their floating dock and to shore, unofficially named Gordon. Later she was beached as a breakwater; this photo probably dates from the 1950s.

The US Navy lend-leased its submarine S.29 (880 tons 1924) to the RN, who commissioned her as P.556 in June 1942. Damaged in a battery explosion, the USN did not want her back, so she was sold to Pounds at Portsmouth in 1947. With their yard at Tipner full of redundant vessels, she was beached off Portchester where her sorry hulk is seen in the photo. She was brought alongside Pounds yard in 1965, but lingered there until her last trace was removed in 1990.

The battleship REVENGE (29,150 tons 1916) after arrival at Inverkeithing. She had been towed from Devonport by ENGLISHMAN, SEAMAN and SUPERMAN at a cost of £5,250, moored off the yard on 4 September 1948. BISCO had allocated the ship to T W Ward Ltd, who could easily handle such large ships. The muzzles of 'A' turret's 15-inch guns have been cut off - perhaps for a publicity photo - as the main demolition did not start until February 1949.

This view from REVENGE's bridge with NELSON alongside was probably taken in late 1949, at the same time as p.3 and p.5. She had previously been moored off the yard. REVENGE yielded 24,955 tons of saleable scrap, plus 2,708 tons of rubbish - concrete, tiles, asbestos etc. The most valuable items were 1,194 tons of non-ferrous metals and 6,072 tons of armour quality nickel steel, plus 17,517 tons of ferrous materials and 172 tons of other saleable items.

Three ships alongside Ward's deep water wharf with its 30ft depth of water - just enough for a lightened battleship. Inboard is the battleship NELSON (33,950 tons 1927) which had arrived from Rosyth on 15 March 1949, after some material had already been removed in the dockyard. Centre is REVENGE, even though she had arrived six months before NELSON. Outboard is the 8,515 grt refrigerated cargo ship PORT ADELAIDE of 1919 which had arrived on 21 August 1949.

Cashmore's shipbreaking yard on the River Usk at Newport was subject to a large tidal range. Indeed the cruiser AJAX (6,985 tons 1935) temporarily grounded on her arrival under tow from lay-up in the River Fal, before berthing on 13 November 1949. Tucked inboard is the hulk of ex-U.3017, taken over by the Admiralty for trials of this Type XXI U-boat after WW2, which had arrived on 25 October.

The cruiser NORFOLK (9,925 tons 1930) arrived at Newport on 19 February 1950, in tow of ENGLISHMAN from lay-up in the River Fal. Note her access gangway at right. The photos and those on p.8 show the general state of a warship laid up with little attempt at preservation.

NORFOLK was broken up by John Cashmore Ltd, under contract to BISCO. Her anti-aircraft armament appears to have been removed before arrival. Her four twin 8-inch Mark II mountings had been made by Vickers-Armstrongs at Barrow at a cost of £500,000, a quarter of her total cost. She yielded 8,532 tons of saleable material.

Another cruiser ARETHUSA (5,220 tons 1935) high but not so dry at Cashmore's yard shortly after arrival on 9 May 1950, which did not require a separate beaching ground to finish hulks off. Five of the scotch derricks typical of British shipbreaking yards can be seen at the river berths, with capacities typically 5 to 10 tons.

The unrecognisable hulk of the submarine depot ship RESOURCE (12,300 tons 1929) at Inverkeithing on 21 September 1954. She had arrived from Portsmouth on 1 February. After lightening at the deep water berth to a draft of 10-15ft, hulks were moved to No. 3 berth for finishing off, as it dried out at low tide.

The aircraft carrier INDEFATIGABLE (26,000 tons 1944) had been laid up in the Gareloch from September 1954, her low 14ft hangar height making her unsuitable for modernisation. After handover to BISCO, she was towed up the Clyde to Dalmuir, berthing at Arnott, Young's yard on 4 November 1956. With no beaching ground at this former Beardmore shipyard, most lightened hulks were towed to the associated yard of West of Scotland Shipbreaking at Troon for final demolition. She arrived there on 2 September 1957 drawing 13ft forward and 9ft aft, and is seen here on 13 September, cut down forward to the level of the lower hangar deck.

INDEFATIGABLE from aft on 13 September 1957, berthed on the north side of the main breakwater. Her four 15ft diameter propellers have already been cut off, each yielding 16 tons of valuable manganese bronze. Such scrap was usually sold back to propeller manufacturers for re-melting, probably to Bull's Metal & Marine at Yoker on the Clyde. The last piece was lifted ashore on 12 April 1959. She produced 23,395 tons of saleable material with a total value of £458,372 and a net value of £326,275 after deducting costs.

INDEFATIGABLE at Troon, also on 13 September 1957. Cut down to lower decks, she is a maze of small compartments, with decks partially cut away to allow the breaker's men access to remove equipment. Moving around decks in such a condition was hazardous, especially if there had been recent rain or frost. The two nearest dark rectangular openings to the right look like the aft boiler room uptakes, which would be trunked across the ship to the funnel on the starboard side.

The battleship ANSON (35,000 tons 1942) was laid up in the Gareloch from mid 1950, along with KING GEORGE V and DUKE OF YORK. Photographed on 25 September 1954, she was under Care & Maintenance by Metal Industries (Salvage) Ltd who operated from the nearby Faslane shipbreaking yard. She was the first of the KGV battleships to be handed over to BISCO, only two days after the Admiralty had advised them that all four were available for scrap. Local tugs including FLYING TEMPEST, FLYING BUZZARD and FLYING TYPHOON moved her alongside Shipbreaking Industries' Faslane's 35ft deep jetty on 17 December 1957.

ANSON at No.1 Berth in March 1958. Just visible at the right is one of her port twin 5.25-inch High Angle/Low Angle (HA/LA) mountings, P.1 - they were numbered 1 to 4 forward to aft, P (port) or S (starboard). Each mounting had a brass identification plate giving the Mark, manufacturer and Registered Number, and usually the year of manufacture. Mountings of a particular Mark were numbered from 1 in a single series, while guns were numbered by their Mark (I also for the 5.25-inch) but in a different series. ANSON's eight mountings were all intended to be made by Harland & Wolff, who had taken over the former gun mounting works of Coventry Ordnance Works at Scotstoun, Glasgow. In the event her forward four were supplied by Vickers-Armstrongs' Scotswood works in Newcastle (Nos.14-17) and the after four from H&W (Nos.30-33). No.30 was P.3.

By March 1958, ANSON's foremast and funnel had been removed, but the main 14-inch director control tower remains, as do the two forward Mark VI high angle directors for her 5.25-inch guns – the only British battleship to get that 1944 design at her refit in Devonport before joining the British Pacific Fleet.

A view on that same March day of the aft side of ANSON's forward superstructure, fore funnel already gone. Her former aircraft hangars (bottom left) have been converted to additional accommodation spaces. It would take another sixteen months to remove her completely from the water.

18

The first of ANSON's 92-ton 14-inch guns on 'Y' turret was cut off in March 1958. By so doing, the heavier breech end would be within the capability of Faslane's 60-ton floating crane. The tallies are from her fire controls.

By mid 1958, ANSON's upperworks and forward forecastle deck structure had gone, cut down to the level of the main deck (top of the main 14-15-inch thick armour belt). The small square hole in her stem is for a chain cable to secure her to the quayside. Six months after arrival, she is riding 5ft higher in the water, after the removal of some 6,500 tons at a cost of about £7 per ton.

ANSON on 29 May 1958, with 'Y' turret's quadruple 14-inch guns and gunhouse removed, leaving the trunnions which supported the gun cradles and the roller path which supported the 1,550 ton revolving weight. The hulk astern is the 22,048 grt liner ASTURIAS.

ANSON's hulk was moved to the beaching ground on 10 March 1959, roughly the site of the present Syncrolift covered drydock at the Trident submarine base. To the left is the port after engine room, driving the port inner shaft. The anti-torpedo side protection system has been cut open to reveal the outer empty compartment, the middle one usually filled with oil fuel or sea water and the inner also empty. Her anti-rolling bilge keel is prominent.

ANSON's hulk on the beaching ground on 22 June 1959. The four propeller shafts (hollow to reduce weight) can be seen each cut off at the bulkhead. Between the inner shafts is 'Y' 14-inch magazine below its shell room. She yielded 30,492 tons of ferrous material, 1982 of non-ferrous, 462 of ferrous re-usables, 184 tons of equipment and sundries, 123 tons of equipment returned to the Admiralty, 434 tons of oil fuel and 1,555 tons of ballast and rubbish, totalling 35,232 tons worth £708,215. After deducting breaking and other costs, there was a net surplus of £458,170, eventually returned to Treasury via BISCO.

The battleship DUKE OF YORK (35,000 tons 1941) alongside at Faslane on 5 March 1958, fifteen days after she had been moved from her moorings in the Gareloch to Shipbreaking Industries' quay. The submarine depot ship ADAMANT lies astern on part of the quay leased to the Admiralty. The charthouse with its brass name tally was immediately abaft the conning tower, whose slits can be seen below the Admiral's bridge with its square windows, which was protected by 3-inch thick non-cemented armour.

FIRE CONTROL RM   HIGH ANGLE CONT POSIT   'Y' SHELL ROOMS

Nº 3 CASEMATE

Another view of DUKE OF YORK on 5 March 1958, probably taken from SI's launch. Demolition work had not yet started, probably to allow equipment to be removed for return to the Admiralty. To this end, lighting circuits below decks were energised, which had helped the author explore the ship a few days earlier. Metal Industries' (Salvage) tug METINDA III lies alongside.

(Left) A selection of armament related compartment name tallies. No.3 casemate housed the 5.25-inch ammunition hoists, seen between the funnels at upper (weather) deck level. 'Y' shell room was beneath the after quadruple turret on the lower platform deck, i.e. one deck above the hold (or inner bottom) which itself housed the 14-inch magazine with its cordite charges. There were four high angle control positions (one for each director) housing the fire control clocks (predictors) on the upper platform deck (one below the lower deck), two immediately ahead of the forward engine rooms and two abaft the after engine rooms. The fire control room tally is bit ambiguous and may refer to what is more correctly termed the transmitting station, right next to the forward HACPs.

DUKE OF YORK from the quayside on 5 March 1958, with demolition work not yet started. One of the 10 ton cargo handling cranes originally installed at Faslane as a WW2 military port is to the right. Her 5.25-inch mountings were Mark I (the Dido class cruisers had Mark II). All eight were made by Harland & Wolff, Nos. 22-29. The plate below was from S.1 mounting Registered No.23.

5.25 INCH H.A/L.A TWIN MARK I	TONS	CWTS.	QRS.
WT. OF MOUNTING WITH WORKING CHAMBER COMPLETE	74	6	0
WT. OF COAMING PLATES	2	0	0
WT. OF BASE RING & ROLLERS	3	7	0
WT. OF CIRCULAR CHUTES	1	3	0
TOTAL WEIGHT	80	16	0

DUKE OF YORK's forward 14-inch 'A' and 'B' mountings on 5 March 1958. Her ten guns had fired a total of 1,265 rounds in 14 actions in WW2. For 14-inch gun mountings, each elevating cradle with slide and gun had a plate giving total weight (125 tons). The gun weight included the balance weight at the breech end to allow the guns to elevate to 40° with the trunnions near the rear of the gun. The right hand cradle of the twin Mark II mounting was numbered 15R. Vickers-Armstrongs Elswick works in Newcastle made her 'A' and 'B' mountings, while Barrow made her quadruple Mark III 'Y' mounting.

The thick side armour reveals this hulk to be a battleship - DUKE OF YORK at Faslane. 14-inch thick cemented (hard faced) armour protected the machinery spaces seen here, with 15-inch over the magazines. It was fitted in three strakes each about 8ft deep; some of the centre strake is still standing. The joints were tongued and grooved to give a secure fit and share the load of shell impact with adjacent plates. The plate itself was bolted at the back through to the main shell plating. Her pitometer log scale suggests a maximum speed of 31 knots, but her best speed in service was 28.

Standing on DUKE OF YORK's main deck (one below the upper deck) and looking forward in the spring of 1959. The remains of the capstan drive are in the centre, with the petty officers heads (WCs) to the right. The anti-mine paravanes streamed from the stem were stowed in this area. Below on the middle deck (one below the main deck) is what is left of the boys' messing space.

The top of the lowest strake of DUKE OF YORK's side armour was almost at the level of the lower deck, just below the waterline. It tapered from 15-inch thick at the top to 5½-inch at the bottom. It typically contained about 4% nickel and 2% chromium, resulting in a scrap price, then, of about £20 per ton, compared with about £11 for mild steel. The growth of mussels suggests that her last drydocking was that at Liverpool in September 1951 - this photo is dated 30 June 1959. She yielded £543,499 to the Treasury - scrap prices had risen since ANSON - or 7.4% of her £7.29M newbuilding cost. It had taken an average of 65 men 120 weeks to demolish her, each paid about 5s per hour (£0.25). The frigate astern is WIGTOWN BAY.

An unrecognisable DUKE OF YORK at Faslane's No. 1 berth on 30 June 1959. Three rail mounted scotch derrick cranes are working the ship. Scrap steel was despatched (not sold by the shipbreaker) to a steelworks nominated by BISCO, often Colville's at Motherwell for SI, the transfer price being kept confidential by BISCO. Battleships and carriers had prison cells for offending sailors needing to be locked up. The KGVs had six forward on the lower deck, the level she is now cut down to, just abaft the cable locker.

DUKE OF YORK's aft end at the level of her lower deck (one below the middle deck) on 30 June 1959, revealing the tips of her 3-bladed 14.5ft diameter propellers. Under the BISCO contract, the shipbreaker sold such non-ferrous items to metal dealers on behalf of BISCO, receiving a commission of 5%. Some tallies from technical compartments: the steering gear compartment with its four hydraulic rams moving the single rudder was below the armoured lower deck immediately above the starboard inner propeller whose tip is just showing. The machine shop was on the middle deck above the after engine rooms. The shipwrights workshop was in the aft superstructure near S.4 5.25-inch mounting. 'A' Boiler Room with its two watertube boilers was below the forward funnel, taking up three decks in height, and entered through an airlock to maintain a higher air pressure.

Aircraft carriers as well as battleships were laid up in the Gareloch in the 1950s. HERCULES' construction was suspended after her machinery by Parsons Marine Steam Turbine Co. had been installed in December 1945 at Vickers-Armstrongs yard on the Tyne. She had cost the Admiralty £1.64M to date, about 80% of expected final cost. She was towed from the Tyne to the Gareloch on 18 July 1946. She was sold to India in February 1957 for completion by Harland & Wolff at Belfast and renamed VIKRANT, so the photo was probably taken in 1956.

The Algerine class minesweeper ROMOLA (900 tons 1945) had been laid up at Devonport in 1956 after service with the Fishery Protection Squadron. It was only a short tow to Demmelweek & Redding's yard in Sutton Pool, Plymouth, on 19 November 1957. Beached on the east side, demolition started at the bow, and a few weeks later has reached just aft of her 4-inch gun. Algerines generally yielded about 700-800 tons of saleable material, with a net value of £10,000-13,000. The area is now redeveloped with marinas, shops and restaurants.

HOWE (35,000 tons 1942) was the only KGV class battleship not laid up in the Gareloch. She was towed by WELSHMAN and ENGLISHMAN for £10,000 from Devonport on 27 May 1958, having had to wait for better weather than her three sisters which were already close to their breakers. Drawing 30ft, she grounded off Inverkeithing harbour for two days before being refloated and berthed at Ward's yard on 4 June. She is seen on 4 August after frigate LARGO BAY had been secured alongside.

Ward's deepwater berth was busy on 4 August with the submarine depot ship MONTCLARE alongside, HOWE as yet uncut, and LARGO BAY having arrived from Portsmouth on 11 July. Only the blue of the sky and water show that despite the grey ships, this really is a colour photograph. Two of HOWE's Mark V high angle directors can be seen above the bridge. The calculating table (an analogue computer) in the HACS took information on the target from the director and worked out the pointing orders to be sent to the 5.25-inch guns.

HOWE's quarterdeck as seen from MONTCLARE also on 4 August. The octuple 2-pdr pom-pom Mark VI (made at Barrow) on 'Y' turret is kooncoted, where a netting was spread over equipment and waterproof plastic sprayed on. Its interior was dehumidified to preserve the equipment from corrosion.

Another view of HOWE's quarterdeck on 4 August, showing 'Y' 14-inch quadruple mounting built by Vickers-Armstrongs at Barrow and erected in February 1942. Such a mounting originally cost about £640,000 including guns, or about 8½% of total ship cost. The two after 5.25-inch directors are also kooncoted.

A close up on 4 August of HOWE's after funnel, part of the port boat crane (originally fitted to handle aircraft) and P.3 twin 5.25-inch mounting. Two kooncoted twin 20mm mountings are abaft the funnel. The identification plate comes from her S.4 mounting, Registered No. 39. Harland & Wolff made all eight of her 5.25-inch mountings (Nos.34-41), easily shipped the 1½ miles upstream to the Fairfield fitting out basin.

Two views of HOWE at Inverkeithing on 4 August 1958 looking forward, showing her reasonably intact state with her teak decking. The latter planks would be carefully removed and sent to shipbreaker Hughes Bolckow at Blyth for making garden furniture.

Ten months later on 22 June 1959, HOWE has been cut down to her main deck (top of side armour belt) and to middle deck level, in a view that would never be seen during construction where main hull structure was complete before the side armour plates were fitted. The thickness of cemented armour will either be 14-inch if this is over machinery spaces or 15-inch if over magazine areas, topped off by a light shedding plate. HOWE yielded 11,661 tons of nickel steel worth £243,013. The 3,066 tons of cemented armour was mostly from the main belt, with much of the 7,840 tons of non-cemented armour from deck and gunhouses. Her guns yielded a further 755 tons.

HOWE's lower deck aft on 22 June 1959, with cabins removed on the port side, but with the shell extending up to the middle deck. A spring loaded armoured hatch cover is open in the centre leading down to stores. Her hulk was beached on 17 September 1959, with scrap recoveries afloat and ashore completed two years later. 33,986 tons were recovered, worth £719,810. The net surplus after costs was £481,354, or 6.6% of her £7.33M newbuilding cost.

Standing on HOWE's forward upper platform deck in the cable locker area looking aft on 22 June 1959. The main bulkhead extending up to the lower deck is the aft boundary to a pump room (port side) with the two valves leading to the 350 ton/hour pump visible. Centre and to starboard are provision rooms. Behind the red bulkhead are fresh water tanks. The engine room platforms were at this same level. In addition to the four sets of one main high pressure and one low pressure steam turbine, the KGVs also had a cruising turbine clutched to the forward end of each HP turbine. These were more economical at low powers, being capable of speeds up to 18 knots, giving an endurance of 5,400 nautical miles.

A nonchalant worker stands on what is left of the HOWE's middle deck forward on 22 June 1959, with the top of the middle armour strake visible. Three men, also without any protective clothing, stand on the lower deck in what was a clothes washing compartment. Behind them is the top of the well stiffened inner torpedo bulkhead protection, two thicknesses of 1¾-inch D.1 quality higher tensile steel. To the left, the white painted space encloses 'A' turret's ammunition hoists. The jumble of oxygen and propane gas pipes only add to the numerous hazards. Beyond is the RFA tanker WAVE COMMANDER which had arrived on 9 May.

MAIN SIGNAL OFFICE

TELEPRINTER ROOM

CRYPTOGRAPHIC OFFICE

Name ship of the class KING GEORGE V moored in the Gareloch on 18 September 1957, with ANSON in the background. Metal Industries (Salvage) had a contract to maintain the battleships, so a launch took workers out each day from Faslane. While there were some signal offices near the bridge, the Main Signal Office was below armour on the lower deck, directly below the mainmast. The Teleprinter Room and Cryptographic Office were adjacent on the middle deck immediately abaft the after armoured transverse bulkhead next to 'Y' barbette, accessed through the midshipmen's sleeping space.

Standing on top of KING GEORGE V's 'A' turret (roof plates 6-inch thick non-cemented armour or 240lb/sq ft) her bows point to Faslane on 18 September 1957 with Orient Lines' OTRANTO to the left, and Royal Mail's ASTURIAS to the right who had arrived four days earlier.

KING GEORGE V's quarterdeck somewhat cleaner than her forecastle on 18 September 1957, with a painting raft in the foreground. The light steel plates on the rear of 'Y' turret cover vent holes. Laid up in the Gareloch since 1950, she had last been drydocked in Liverpool in 1955.

KING GEORGE V on an overcast 18 September 1957 in the Gareloch. Her 14-inch gunports have been sealed. All her close range AA guns have been removed. She was moved to an anchorage at Tail of the Bank on 8 January 1958, then towed up the Clyde to Dalmuir on 20 January. Some of her compartment tallies were made in aluminium rather than brass. While there was a steering position in the conning tower (immediately below the crest on the bridge front), the Lower Steering Position was eight decks below on the upper platform deck, which was protected by the 6-inch thick armoured main deck. The two positions were connected by a 65ft long communication tube 1½-inch thick. The Damage Control Room was directly above the LSP.

KING GEORGE V at Arnott, Young's yard at Dalmuir on 3 May 1958. All her superstructure has gone. 'Y' quadruple turret (built by Vickers-Armstrongs at Elswick) is well demolished, showing just how thick her 14-inch gun bodies were. The Transmitting Station controlling the 14-inch guns was in the same area as the lower steering position, containing a Mark IX Admiralty Fire Control Table made by Elliott Brothers, who later made digital computers. The forward 5.25-inch magazines were on the two decks immediately below, capable of stowing some 4,500 rounds (560 each gun). There were two HACPs next to the TS and two more on the same level further aft between the after engine rooms and 'Y' shell room.

The burner is cutting 'Y' turret's left hand 14-inch gun breech end horizontally on 3 May. With only a 30-ton capacity crane, the 92 ton guns had to be cut into several pieces. The 13-inch thick front plates (520lb) also had to be cut into smaller pieces - a process which lost about 2% of the weight. The barbette armour was also 13-inch thick, although reduced to 12-inch near the centreline, where there was a lesser probability of a hit. Her net sale proceeds from 33,717 tons of recycled material amounted to £467,065.

5·25 INCH HA/LA TWIN MARK I
VICKERS–ARMSTRONGS PATTERN

MADE BY VICKERS ARMSTRONGS ELSWICK 1940	TONS	CWTS	QRS
WT OF CARRIAGE & TURNTABLE	18	5	0
WT OF GUNHOUSE REAR	6	9	1
FRONT	9	18	3
WT OF BASE RING & ROLLERS	3	7	0
WT OF WORKING CHAMBER	7	2	0
WT OF HOISTS	3	12	
ADMY REGD No 11			

5·25 INCH H.A./L.A. TWIN MARK I

WT. OF MOUNTING WITH	TONS	CWTS	QRS
WORKING CHAMBER COMPLETE	74	6	0
WT. OF COAMING PLATES	2	0	0
WT. OF BASE RING & ROLLERS	3	7	0
WT. OF CIRCULAR CHUTES	1	3	0
TOTAL WEIGHT	80	16	0

KGV still recognisable at Dalmuir, although about 2ft lighter at the bow - every 120 tons removed reduced her draft by about one inch. She is in what was formerly the fitting out basin of the Beardmore shipyard which closed in 1931. KGV's hulk was towed to be finished off at Troon on 20 May 1959, drawing only 9ft 4in forward and 8ft aft corresponding to a displacement of about 10,000 tons. Each 5.25-inch mounting had two identification/weight plates, one for the complete weight of each Mark I mounting and one for the weights of replaceable parts. The latter shows that this P.3 mounting was Registered No.11, the upper aftermost one in the photo. As production of these complex mountings was slower than expected, four of PRINCE OF WALES' eight mountings being built by Vickers-Armstrongs at Barrow were diverted to KGV, to become her forward mountings (Nos. 2-5 - No.1 was the trial mounting in IRON DUKE). Their Elswick works only made four mountings (KGV Nos. 10-13), Barrow eight (4 KGV, 4 PRINCE OF WALES), Scotswood four for ANSON, Harland & Wolff the remaining 24 (4 PoW, 8 DoY, 4 ANSON, 8 HOWE).

Maintenance aircraft carrier PERSEUS (12,265 tons 1945) had been laid up in the Gareloch in 1957 after plans to convert her to a submarine depot ship at Harland & Wolff, Belfast had been cancelled. She was handed over to BISCO and towed the short distance to Smith & Houston's yard at Port Glasgow on 6 May 1958, this view being taken on 5 August. Their ships were usually berthed stern first and demolished from aft to forward, being hauled up the beach as they were lightened. The yard was formerly part of the Clyde Shipbuilding & Engineering shipyard which closed in 1928.

A second view of PERSEUS, also taken on 5 August 1958, shows her twin propeller shafts and bossings (most large RN warships had open shafts supported by 'A' brackets), with her 14ft diameter 10 ton propellers already removed. She yielded 542 tons of non-ferrous metals, which made up 30% of her £163,542 sales value from 9,449 tons recovered. Net value was £105,832. Her sister PIONEER was broken up at Inverkeithing in 1954.

The Dido class cruiser CLEOPATRA (5,450 tons 1941) on the mud at Cashmore's Newport yard on 7 February 1959. She had arrived on 15 December 1958 from Portsmouth, where she had been in reserve since 1954, initially as flagship of the then large Reserve Fleet.

CLEOPATRA on 7 February 1959, Left: both funnels down, and showing her 3-inch side armour belt. Right: her quarterdeck strewn with pipes and cables.

CLEOPATRA's forward two twin 5.25-inch turrets with their kooncoting protection. The third 'Q' turret had been removed in 1944 at Philadelphia where she was being repaired after torpedo damage off Malta on 16 July 1943. All five of her 5.25-inch mountings were made by Vickers-Armstrongs' Scotswood works in 1940-41.

CLEOPATRA's name in brass letters on her after portside superstructure. Brass items were usually sorted and sold as non-ferrous scrap, but any of special interest might be sold to collectors. Indeed Tom Ferrers-Walker had a large collection of such at his home in Birmingham, possibly even including these letters. The breakers would normally charge little more than scrap value of the brass if no work was involved, or even nothing for small items like the compartment tally for the Forward Engine Room.

CLEOPATRA on 7 February 1959 looking forward at Cashmore's yard, with its high tidal range. She yielded 4,901 tons of saleable material worth £125,642, plus 688 tons of oil fuel, ballast and rubbish. Net value after demolition costs was £82,851, or 5.1% of her £1.62M newbuilding cost. The hulk ahead is probably the 17,700grt liner REINA DEL PACIFICO.

A close up of CLEOPATRA's bridge on 7 February 1959. Internal fittings, furniture and woodwork would be stripped to reduce the fire risk before cutting the steel structure; some could also be resold if in good condition. Sometimes items had to be returned to the Admiralty for storage and spares - the rectangular hole in the side of the bridge is probably to remove some electrical equipment.

DIDO, name ship of her cruiser class (5,450 tons 1940) lies alongside Ward's Anchor Line Dock berth at Barrow in August 1958, shortly after her arrival from Portsmouth in tow of WELSHMAN on 16 July. Her prominent external degaussing cable is still visible, fitted internally on later ships. Her Cammell Laird engine builder's plate is inset – Admiralty ships were rarely fitted with a hull builder's plate. Also inset is the identification plate off one of her four 300kW turbo-generators. Allen of Bedford was one of the Admiralty's preferred suppliers of auxiliary machinery such as steam and diesel generators, pumps, fans and electric motors.

Ward's were sympathetic at the time in allowing warship enthusiast photographers on board ships for breaking - at their own risk! Left: Looking aft from DIDO's bridge with a kooncoted quadruple 2-pdr prominent. Right: 'X' and 'Y' 5.25-inch twin turrets also kooncoted, made by Vickers-Armstrongs' nearby Barrow works. She yielded 4,669 tons of saleable material.

As well as battleships and carriers, BISCO allocated a proportion of smaller warships to Shipbreaking Industries. The frigate (ex corvette) FLINT CASTLE (1,060 tons 1943) is alongside the hulk of ANSON, having arrived from Devonport on 10 July. She was moved to the beach at Faslane on 18 August, but work was not finally completed until March 1959. It took only one ship burner to cut her down for the four shore burners to reduce the blocks to furnace size. Her sister CARISBROOKE CASTLE was also broken up at Faslane at the same time – see photo of her 4-inch gun in *To Sail No More Part 1*. As most of the Castles were not built by regular warship builders, the Admiralty procured much of their machinery for allocation to shipbuilders as production required. So her main 4 cylinder triple expansion steam reciprocating engine was made by George Clark of Sunderland, installed by Caledon of Dundee (Contract 614) who also built her hull (Contract 411) while her two watertube oil-fired boilers were built by Cammell Laird. Her boiler pressure test plate shows 387 lb/sq in compared with a working pressure of 225. It was tested by Lloyds Register, who oversaw construction of many smaller naval vessels, on 22 July 1943, ready for installation in the hull launched on 31 July.

FLINT CASTLE shows her 4-inch Mark XXIII mounting to advantage - this now obsolete weapon was not required to be returned to the Admiralty. The Castle class generally yielded about 840-920 tons of material with a net value of £10-12,000. The Castles were the first escorts to deploy the new ahead throwing anti-submarine mortar Squid in any number. It was fitted on the deck above her 4-inch, connected via a hoist to the magazine in the hold, which held 81 projectiles (27 salvoes). This plate from LAUNCESTON CASTLE (broken up at St Davids on the Forth) shows that the compartment was between Frames 35 and 41 - RN warships numbered their frames from forward unlike merchant ships from aft.

SQUID PROJLE ROOM FRS 35-41

REVS.	KNOTS.
118	7
127	8
137	9
147	10
158	11
170	12
184	13
199	14
215	15
232	16
250	17
269	18
289	19
299	19·5

As well as Faslane, Shipbreaking Industries operated two smaller yards on the Forth, one in the north-west corner of Rosyth Dockyard, and one at Charlestown two miles to the west. The Black Swan class frigate SPARROW (1,430 tons 1946) is seen at low tide at the latter in June 1958, having arrived from Portsmouth on 26 May in tow of MASTERMAN. Her main armament consisted of three twin 4-inch Mk XIX mountings. They were designed by Vickers-Armstrongs, but such was the demand for these high angle guns that general engineering companies were also brought in to manufacture many in WW2. The plate shows that Registered Number 726 was built by Marshall, Sons & Co of Gainsborough, who normally made agricultural machinery. The weight shown excludes guns. Also shown is the Speed-RPM table from the bridge. Speed changes were ordered to the engine room by propeller revolutions per minute, so such a table was needed. The Black Swans were designed for 19.5 knots fully loaded and clean at 300 rpm.

SPARROW had moved to the Charlestown demolition berth by 4 August 1958. Black Swans generally yielded about 1000-1050 tons of saleable material with a net value of £15-17,000, or about 5% of newbuilding cost. Her engine builder's plate shows Denny engine contract 1128 (although her hull contract was 1385). Unusually one of her (two) boiler test plates bears the ship's name. It was tested to 50% above normal working pressure of 250 lb/sq in.

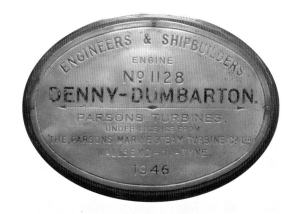

Still at the Charlestown layby berth in June 1958, the Hunt class destroyer LEDBURY (1,050 tons 1942) inboard with her twin 4-inch guns removed by the Admiralty, having arrived from Portsmouth on 12 May. She was transferred to Rosyth for demolition on 1 July. SPARROW is outboard.

The 'S' class submarine SLEUTH (715 tons 1944) well cut down alongside SI's Charlestown yard on 25 June 1959. She had arrived from lay-up in the Forth on 15 September 1958. 'S' class submarines generally yielded 500-600 tons of saleable material, with a net value of £10-12,000 - the higher figures if the battery with its lead was still aboard.

The submarine depot ship MONTCLARE (20,000 tons full load 1922) had been laid up at Portsmouth since 1955. She had been converted from a P&O liner in 1942. BISCO allocated her to Ward's Inverkeithing yard, where she arrived in tow of ENGLISHMAN and WELSHMAN (for £5,000) on 3 February 1958 after a six day voyage. The view here on 7 March is from Inverkeithing town across the main railway line, with alongside her the Cunarder SCYTHIA.

Two views of MONTCLARE at Inverkeithing on 7 March 1958. Left: starboard side looking forward. Right: her two funnels, both used for her main boilers unlike the Admiralty designed depot ships where only the aft funnel was for their boilers, the forward one for workshop exhausts. Her outturn was 10,721 tons of saleable material plus 2,155 tons of pig iron ballast worth £13 per ton and 1,595 tons of rubbish.

The Town class cruiser LIVERPOOL (9,400 tons 1938) at 591ft was about the longest ship that P & W MacLellan could handle at their yard at Boness. She had been a living ship for the Reserve Fleet at Portsmouth since 1952. She was towed from there by WELSHMAN for £4,000 on 27 June 1958 arriving at Boness on 2 July. This photo must have been taken shortly afterwards, with a token piece cut off her bow.

LIVERPOOL's two forward triple 6-inch Mk XXIII turrets (built by Vickers-Armstrongs at Barrow) still looking in reasonable condition - and full of valuable non-ferrous metal.

Looking across LIVERPOOL's quarterdeck to the north side of the Firth of Forth. Some teak planking has been lifted for possible resale.

LIVERPOOL's aft end buried in the mud on 25 June 1959, a year after arrival. It is low tide - a tide mark on the hull shows the level of high tide. Two identification plates from her triple 6-inch 'Y' mounting. The right hand plate refers to the whole revolving structure weighing 164.5 tons, light enough to be lifted complete except for guns by her builder's (Fairfield) fitting out crane. The elevating part of each gun had its own plate as it was replaceable, so needed to be traceable with the plate showing that it was on the right gun of Mounting No.26 - about 35 in all were manufactured including spares.

The muddy berth at Boness with no proper quay was not the ideal site for shipbreaking, although it had been in use since 1892. The shore derrick cranes provided poor coverage of the hulls, so one has been erected on LIVERPOOL's upper deck on 25 June 1959.

The unrecognisable remains of LIVERPOOL on 9 June 1960. It took until March 1961 to recover all the material - as long as it had taken Fairfield's to build her - admittedly using many more men. She did however yield 6,954 tons of ferrous scrap, 671 of non-ferrous and 297 tons of other saleable items, totalling 7,922 tons, worth £210,158. Her net value after costs was £145,026, slightly more than sisters NEWCASTLE and GLASGOW, or 7.8% of her £1.85M newbuilding cost.

The chaos of one shipbreaking yard, with what looks like a main seawater circulating pump in LIVERPOOL's engine room area, and remains of her Asdic (sonar) dome and torpedo tubes on the beach. The smoke may come from burning oil fuel residues ignited by a burner's torch.

Maintenance carrier UNICORN (14,750 tons 1943) had been laid up in the Hamoaze at Devonport after returning from Korea in November 1953. In this view, she is probably in Extended Reserve, i.e. unmanned and not expected for further service.

Two views of UNICORN at the breakers on the Clyde on 29 June 1959. Demolition of the island has started, with the after 4-inch high angle/low angle director platform cut away and allowed to fall on the flight deck where it could be dragged within reach of the crane ashore.

UNICORN berthed stern first in the former Beardmore fitting out basin at Dalmuir on 29 June 1959. She had been allocated by BISCO to Arnott, Young and towed from Devonport on 11 June by WELSHMAN and TRADESMAN. She berthed at Dalmuir on 15 June, assisted by five Clyde tugs. The stern opening was designed to stow an aircraft carrying lighter.

Another view on 29 June 1959 of UNICORN with the 150-ton ex-Beardmore fitting out crane across the basin. The rail wagons at left will be loaded with scrap for steel-works at Motherwell.

The typical jumble of a scrapyard with parts of UNICORN lying on the dockside on 29 June 1959, including part of her aircraft handling crane, lifted off by Arnott, Young's 30-ton travelling crane.

UNICORN's forward flight deck almost projecting into the River Clyde on 29 June 1959. Her single hydraulic catapult track is to the left, and to the right an empty platform for one of her twin 4-inch guns.

This unrecognisable hulk is UNICORN at Troon on 9 June 1960, with 4-inch ammunition stowage racks to the right. As with other large ships started at Dalmuir, the lightened hulk had been towed to Troon for beaching and completion on 29 March, drawing only 8ft. She yielded 13,536 tons of saleable material worth a net £180,730, after the last section was lifted ashore on 23 November 1960.

The trials cruiser CUMBERLAND (10,000 tons 1928) had been used in the 1950s to test the 6-inch and 3-inch guns and fire control systems for the Tiger class cruisers. After a short lay-up at Devonport, she arrived at Cashmore's yard at Newport on 3 November 1959, with her armament removed. She is seen here 18 days later, with demolition well under way.

CUMBERLAND on 21 November 1959 showing her three funnels, the last such class of British cruiser. Forward, chunks of her bow structure have been parked on the forecastle and 'B' gun deck.

CUMBERLAND alongside Cashmore's River Usk yard on 21 November 1959. The sidelights indicate that no belt armour covers her upper machinery spaces.

CUMBERLAND at Newport on 21 November 1959. At that time, cruisers displayed their pendant number (C57); somewhat superfluous as a recognition feature, given her distinctive profile.

CUMBERLAND's quarterdeck on 21 November 1959. It had been cut down one deck in 1936 to save topweight for new anti-aircraft armament and an aircraft hangar.

Looking into CUMBERLAND'S 'B' barbette and ring bulkhead which had supported the new twin 6-inch Mark XXVI mounting being trialled in place of the original twin 8-inch. She yielded 8,277 tons of saleable materials (plus 1,004 tons of ballast and rubbish) worth a net £139,390.

Two frigates at Faslane on 23 June 1959: inboard the Hunt class WHADDON (907 tons built 1941 as a destroyer) who arrived 5 April and outboard the Bay class WIGTOWN BAY (1,580 tons 1946) who arrived on 13 April. Both had been laid up in reserve in South Wales ports, where redundant coal loading berths were available. Few RN warships carried a hull builder's plate, although an engine builder's plate was usually fitted in the engine room. Harland & Wolff did however sometimes fit a hull plate even if this one from WIGTOWN BAY carries no ship name or hull number (1260) or even year.

A stern view on 23 June 1959: WIGTOWN BAY (left) yielded 1,153 tons of saleable material, with a net value of £14,436. WHADDON yielded only 963 tons but a net value of £24,595 on account the amount of non-ferrous in her destroyer type machinery. Several of the South Wales laid up Hunts had been painted a grey colour which went pinkish. The bow to the left is probably oiler ENNERDALE.

The Hunt class destroyer WILTON (1,050 tons 1942) had arrived on 4 December 1959, having been HQ ship of the Reserve Fleet at Cardiff. She was moved to the beach on 16 May 1960, and is seen here on 7 June. The hulk behind is probably BUCHAN NESS. Every gun mounting needed an identification plate, with its unique registered number (guns were numbered in a different series). This one, unusually cast in lead, shows that her quadruple 2-pdr Mk VII*P (i.e. a powered rather than hand worked mounting) was made in Canada. Dominion Engineering built 50 of the hand operated mountings during WW2 and 178 of the power operated ones. Each of the latter cost about C$40,000, or about £10,000, roughly double the price of one built in the UK.

WILTON's engine room looking forward on 7 June. Lagged steam pipes from the boiler rooms can be seen at the top, gauges on the starting platform at centre, and lower the large diameter pipes taking seawater to the condensers. The steam turbines, condensers and gearing have already been removed. She yielded 970 tons with a net value of £22,895 or about 6½% of newbuilding cost.

A composite view of WILTON on the beaching ground on 7 June 1960. Top left, a general bow view. Top right, the stem. Bottom left looking aft with the circular support to the forward twin 4-inch to the left. Bottom right showing hatches to the two boiler rooms, beyond them the engine room, all with decks removed. Demolition of a Hunt took about 15,000 manhours, only 2% of that required to build one.

It is not entirely clear which end is which on this submarine on the beaching ground at Faslane, but it is bows to the left, with a torpedo tube opening the giveaway. 'V' class VULPINE (545 tons 1944) had been loaned to the Danish Navy in 1947 as STØREN and returned in 1958. She was actually broken under that name, berthing on 29 April 1959. Her two sisters SPRINGEREN (ex P.52) and SÆLEN (ex VORTEX) had preceded her at Faslane. The 30 ton derrick crane hovers over her; there were also three 12 ton cranes at the beach.

This aft section of STØREN shows just how small the 'V' and 'U' class submarines were with a maximum pressure hull diameter of only 16ft (modern nuclear submarines are 37ft) and internal ballast tanks (welded), although the diameter has tapered to about 10ft at this after section. 'X' compensating tank is beneath the deck of the steering gear compartment. The aft hydroplanes actuator is in the centre. The starboard shaft bracket and 4ft 3in diameter propeller is still attached to the hull. She yielded 486 tons with a net value of £11,195. It took an average of only four men 36 weeks to demolish her.

It was not easy to get good outboard photos of ships being broken up at Inverkeithing, as this shot across the main railway line north of fleet oiler WAVE COMMANDER (8,141 grt 1944) demonstrates. She had arrived on 9 May 1959, BISCO having paid £63,000 for her, or a high 16.3% of her newbuilding cost of £387,000 as EMPIRE PAL-ADIN.

The opportunity to see Britain's last battleship VANGUARD (44,500 tons 1946) close up was always a draw on sightseeing Portsmouth harbour boat trips. She had been flagship of the Reserve Fleet since she arrived from Devonport in November 1956, also carrying out some training duties. She cost about £310,000 a year to maintain and man in this role. Moored up harbour she was being readied here on 3 August 1960 for her final voyage to the breakers the next day.

Unlike the King George Vs, VANGUARD had already been sold outright to BISCO, for £540,000. On 4 August 1960, dockyard tugs brought her from her moorings off Hardway to the entrance to Portsmouth harbour. As she reached the narrows, she veered to port and grounded off Point, despite dropping both anchors. These four views show the tugs struggling to pull her off.

Another four shots, with the paddles of GRINDER thrashing the water to port, and CAPABLE and ANTIC pulling from her starboard bow. After ¾ hour she was pulled off, and handed over to the deep sea tugs SAMSONIA and ADVICE in Spithead for the tow to Faslane.

Five days later on 9 August VANGUARD enters the narrows at Rhu at the entrance to the Gareloch, having handed over to local tugs at Tail of the Bank - CAMPAIGNER centre.

VANGUARD being nudged alongside Shipbreaking Industries wharf at Faslane by Steel & Bennie tugs, drawing 28 ft forward, the white telltale at her stem showing that she had not taken on any water since leaving Portsmouth. Her anchors were then being retrieved from the bottom of Portsmouth harbour – a loss of scrap value. Once a ship had arrived at the breakers, they opened up all the compartments, if necessary using keys found on board with their name tallies, to assess saleable material, to check for flammable material that might endanger cutting from an adjoining compartment and for ventilation.

At 1500 on 9 August VANGUARD was secured at her final resting place, SI's deep water Berth No.1. 3-pdr Hotchkiss quick firing guns were used as anti-torpedo boat weapons in the 1890s. Later they were used as saluting guns firing blanks and sub-calibre guns inserted into the breech of large calibre guns for practice. She had four such guns, with the plate off one of them showing that it had been made at the Royal Carriage Department, Woolwich Arsenal in 1893.

Amidst much press interest, reporters and photographers were invited aboard to watch the symbolic cutting off of a 15-inch Mark I gun barrel from 'A' turret. It will take another 22 months to remove her last section from the water.

On the next day, 10 August, the pressmen have departed, and VANGUARD has been shorn of the muzzles of both of 'A' turret's guns. As seen from inside the turret, they were Left gun Registered No. 65 (made by Armstrong, Elswick) and Right gun No. 77 (Vickers, Sheffield).

VANGUARD's 'A' and 'B' turrets have been opened up on 3 September 1960 and the guns removed - 'B' had Left No. 105 and Right No. 108 (both Vickers, Sheffield made in 1916). Samples have been taken of the gunhouse armour for analysis, each plate being given a number. The scrap value was greatly affected by the nickel content. The front and sides had cemented armour with typically 4% nickel, while the 6-inch thick roof was non-cemented. Teak deck planking is neatly stacked for despatch to sister company Hughes Bolckow at Blyth. 3 September was a Saturday, when the yard worked only mornings; this photo was probably taken after the men had gone home.

With the muzzles cut off, the breech end of each 15-inch gun could be lifted out by the 60-ton floating crane. They have been placed ashore on 3 September for dismantling to remove the non-ferrous of the breech mechanisms, before the steel is cut further and sent for re-melting.

The breech end of one of the 15-inch guns. Each breech face was stamped with the Registered Number, the maker's initials and the date of manufacture – but the photo is not clear enough to reveal which gun this is. The location is roughly that of the present Trident and Astute class submarine berths.

VANGUARD's 'X' and 'Y' turrets have been opened up on 3 September 1960 and armour plates marked. The remains of 'X' turret guns have yet to be lifted out: Right No.30 (Coventry Ordnance Works) and Left No.63 (Armstrong, Elswick). 'Y' guns were No. 21 (Left) and 24 (Right) both by Beardmore. The ammunition hoists for her 15-inch guns lifted shell (projectile) and cordite (propellant) separately from shell room and magazine, as these tallies suggest.

By 20 March 1961, demolition has reached the middle deck (left) and revealed the top strake of the side armour and deck armour at main deck level. The remains of S.2 5.25-inch casemate gunbay and gunhouse give an idea of the complexity of the ammunition supply, from the main magazines low in the ship to hoists up to the upper deck casemates. The plates show that they are of the Mark I* pattern with remote power control system RP.10 – the KGVs as built had the Mark I version, see page 50. One plate gives the total revolving weight of nearly 106 tons, much heavier than the Mark I due to RPC as well as a heavier gunhouse, made of 1½ and 2¼-inch non-cemented armour. All eight twin mountings (Reg Nos.1-8) were manufactured at Barrow as confirmed by the cradle plate. They were shipped to John Brown in January and February 1946 in the coaster EMPIRE JACK who made four voyages, each with one mounting in No.1 and one in No.2 hold.

Cut down to middle deck level aft on 20 March, VANGUARD is riding much higher in the water as shown by the white telltale. BISCO recorded that by the end of March 14,542 tons of ferrous material (out of 36,637) had been recovered. The test plate from boiler B.1 (i.e. one of the two in her port forward boiler room) is dated 21 October 1943 - Trafalgar Day! This was a full year before her launch, which suggests that machinery building at John Brown was running ahead of hull construction. The brazed on piece showing a test date of 1955 was at the time of her last refit at Devonport.

VANGUARD no longer recognisable as a battleship in October 1961 - although her four propellers do suggest a large ship. They are revealed as 4 bladed, 14.5ft diameter and weighing 14.25 tons, so probably realised about £3,000 each.

The very last piece of VANGUARD on 4 June 1962, a section of double bottom oil fuel tank, with attached valve, revealing that much of her structure was riveted. She had been beached on 2 April. VANGUARD's final outturn was 36,074 tons of ferrous worth £522,138, 1910 tons of non-ferrous worth £249,621, 816 tons of ferrous re-usables and sundries worth £26,792. Total saleable 38,800 tons worth £798,551. After deducting breaking costs of £5 12s per ton recovered, carriage and purchase price, BISCO made a loss of £20,194. SI recorded that 41,245 tons were removed in all but this included debris, rubbish and oil fuel as well as recyclable material.

The Town class cruiser BIRMINGHAM (9,100 tons 1937) had paid off at Devonport in December 1959. After only a short period in reserve, she was sold to BISCO (as opposed to being handed over and later sales proceeds returned to the Admiralty) for £146,000. She was allocated to T W Ward's Inverkeithing yard where she arrived in tow of TYPHOON and SUPERMAN on 7 September 1960. She had been well cut down here by April 1961. The top of the 4½-inch armour belt is seen at bottom right. She had four sets of machinery each driven by steam turbines which could be supplied from four boilers if cross-connected. Although her hull was built by Devonport Dockyard, it did not manufacture main machinery, which was supplied by John Brown. The test plate from one of the two boilers in the forward boiler room indicates that the working pressure was 350 lb/sq in (50% test overload) and was tested six months before the machinery was shipped from Clydebank, in the coaster GREYFRIARS on 17 September 1936, having taken three days to load.

Two views of BIRMINGHAM taken in April 1961 from the liner BRITANNIC berthed outboard. She has been cut down to the lower deck (two below the forecastle deck) forward and aft. Midships in the left view, the main deck still covers the machinery spaces. The right view shows that the steering gear has already been removed. She yielded 7721 tons of saleable material with a gross value of £205,845. After deduction of sale price and demolition costs – BISCO had agreed with Ward a fixed price of £6-10s per ton recovered – there was a profit of £2,283.

The cruiser JAMAICA (8,530 tons 1942) had been laid up in the Gareloch in November 1957, with little attempt at preservation, indicating that she was not expected for further service; photo 13 June 1960. Like all the Colonies, she had four twin 4-inch Mk XIX mountings. To counter increasingly severe air attacks as the war progressed, such mountings needed to be upgraded to remote power control, whereby the mountings followed the director automatically (and with faster training and elevating speeds) rather than the gunlayer and trainer following electrical pointers. The identification plate shows that this is a new mounting with the RP.52 system. Such mountings were made by Vickers-Armstrongs Scotswood works, and were probably installed at JAMAICA's refit at Portsmouth October 1944 to May 1945. The weight excludes the gun and elevating parts, which were removable.

JAMAICA had been allocated by BISCO to Arnott, Young. She arrived at their Dalmuir yard on 20 December 1960, but seen here in March 1961 alongside cruiser SUPERB.

JAMAICA at Dalmuir on 16 March 1961. Her 'A' and 'B' triple 6-inch gun turrets had been made by Vickers-Armstrongs at Barrow (also her shipbuilders), erected early in 1942.

JAMAICA's transom stern (which increased speed slightly at higher powers) on 16 March 1961. She is drawing about 16ft aft in light condition, compared with 20½ft fully loaded.

JAMAICA on 16 March 1961, showing that nothing external has yet been stripped, either by the Admiralty or by the breakers. 'X' triple 6-inch turret was replaced by light anti-aircraft guns in 1944, now two twin 40mm Bofors Mark V.

JAMAICA's 'Y' turret on 16 March 1961. This triple 6-inch Mark XXIII was made at Barrow (Registered Number 36) with a revolving weight of 170 tons. It was shipped by the shipyard's 150 ton crane in the form of the gunhouse and attached ammunition hoists, then the three guns (weighing 7 tons each) then the gunhouse roof. The quarterdeck has no planking.

Two more on board views of JAMAICA on 16 March 1961. Her bridge was enclosed at her 1956 refit at Chatham.

JAMAICA's two forward 6-inch turrets, hacked open to allow guns and equipment to be removed. The 6-inch gunhouses had protective plating (2-inch on face and roof, 1-inch on sides and rear) rather than armour as in battleships.

Like most Dalmuir hulks, JAMAICA was towed to Troon, arriving at the associated West of Scotland Shipbreaking yard on 30 May 1962, drawing 11ft 6in aft and 3ft 6in forward. Here on 8 June, the side armour has been removed but not the four valuable propellers. She yielded 7,403 tons of saleable material with a net value of £119,856, or 5.8% of her newbuilding cost of £2.08M.

JAMAICA's stem at Troon on 8 June 1962. The marine growth suggests that she had not been drydocked since being taken out of service in 1957. The holes in the stem are for deploying the paravane anti-mine gear. She had now been cut down to the level of the magazines and corresponding handing rooms supplying the hoists.

Cruiser SUPERB (8,800 tons 1945) was also laid up in the Gareloch from 1957, as seen here on 10 June 1960. She too made the voyage to Arnott, Young at Dalmuir arriving on 8 August.

By 21 March 1961, SUPERB is well cut down, mostly to lower deck level. 'B' barbette has been cleared of the 6-inch mounting, while some of ammunition hoist machinery is still visible in 'A' barbette.

A view on the same day looking at SUPERB's aft end from JAMAICA. The forward engine room has been exposed with its mass of asbestos lagged pipework. At that time, the hazards of working with asbestos were not fully understood, so no precautions were being taken during its removal.

SUPERB from aft on 21 March 1961, riding high in the water and soon to be towed to Troon. JAMAICA alongside has been barely touched.

A close up of the SUPERB's forward engine room pipework on 21 March 1961. It is easy to see why extracting valuable non-ferrous from such ships was a labour intensive business. The ship's side to port still extends to the upper deck, probably to make access to JAMAICA easier.

SUPERB's hulk was towed to Troon on 16 May 1961, and beached drawing 10ft 9in aft but only 3ft 6in forward, so she was afloat at high tide (with her propellers below this waterline) but more or less dry at low tide. As required ship speed was signalled to the engine room by propeller revolutions per minute, the bridge needed a conversion table of Speed-RPM. The speeds given are for no paravanes streamed and Asdic dome raised. The brass plate shows the effect of months out of drydock, where each extra three months added about 2 rpm to maintain speed - although the figure engraved of 266 for 29 knots 6 months out of dock is an error for 286. In this condition she required her full 80,000 shp burning 23.8 tons of oil per hour giving her an endurance of 2,200 nautical miles.

A year later, on 8 June 1962, SUPERB's after boiler room and engine room have yet to be cleared. The double hull structure not only provided some protection from damage but was used to store oil fuel. Her outturn was 6,641 tons of ferrous scrap, 777 of non-ferrous and 273 of re-usables and sundries, totalling 7,691 tons, with a gross value of £192,665 and a net value after costs of £128,655.

SUPERB's stern has been demolished up to 'Y' turret by 8 June 1962, with rough draft marks painted on the bulkhead. The severed starboard inner propeller shaft can be seen at right. The last piece was removed on 30 August 1962, just over two years from demolition starting. Meantime work switched to JAMAICA's newly arrived hulk.

The Black Swan class frigate OPOSSUM's (1,470 tons 1945) last voyage was only five miles from her lay-up trot in the Hamoaze to Sutton Pool at Plymouth. She arrived at Demmelweek & Redding's yard on 26 April 1960, so this view with bow demolished would have been taken a few weeks afterwards. She yielded 986 tons of saleable material with a net value of £17,674.

Ward's yard at Inverkeithing was one of the few that BISCO used that could handle the largest ships. Light fleet carrier GLORY (13,190 tons 1945) arrived from her lay-up buoy in the Firth of Forth on 23 August 1961, drawing 18ft. She is lying at Ward's deep water berth on 24 October, outboard of Eagle Oil's tanker SAN LEOPOLDO (10,669 grt built in 1944 as a T2 tanker). The inboard hulk is probably the Shell tanker LINGULA, which had arrived on 20 July.

BEWARE OF PROPELLERS

The forward end of GLORY's flight deck on 24 October 1961. It looks as if her 45 x 34ft forward aircraft lift has been lowered, perhaps to make it easier to remove equipment, or maybe removed as a spare for one of her sisters, as several remained in service with overseas navies.

During GLORY's four year lay-up, grass began to grow on the flight deck! Her last refit had been at Rosyth in 1955-56, costing about £700,000. Her after aircraft lift has also been lowered or removed.

On 31 May 1962 GLORY was moved to Berth No.3 for finishing. The last piece was lifted ashore on 19 September 1962, 56 weeks after she had arrived. The material had all been recycled by July 1963.

GLORY at the finishing berth on 5 June 1962. She yielded 10,872 tons (9,983tons ferrous, 510 non ferrous, 379 other) with a net value of £112,039, or about 5½% of her newbuilding cost. The carrier to the left is THESEUS, having arrived from Portsmouth on 29 May.

The 'Co' class destroyer COSSACK (1,710 tons 1945) at Troon on 15 March 1961, 13 days after arriving from reserve at Devonport. The brass plate shows the settings for lining up the sights in the Mark 6 director for her 4.5-inch guns (which have been removed), seen above the bridge with its two nacelles for Type 275 radar. Across from the West of Scotland Shipbreaking yard was the now closed Ailsa shipyard.

One of COSSACK's name boards has been posed on board BP tanker BRITISH HARMONY – perhaps for sale to a former crew member. The letters look to be wood rather than brass. Passenger-vehicle ferry CERDIC FERRY is being fitted out by the Ailsa shipyard in the background.

Two on board views of COSSACK on 15 March 1961, stripped of many of her fittings. She was moved to the beach on 7 April, where she was finished on 10 May 1962. She yielded 1,167 tons of ferrous scrap worth £12,995, 178 tons of non-ferrous worth £22,767 and 103 tons of other re-usables worth £3,146. The total recycled was 1,448 tons worth £38,908, with a profit to BISCO of £5,185 after a purchase price of £22,250 and demolition and other costs of £11,473.

The small harbour of St Davids, a mile north-east of Inverkeithing but accessed down a dirt track, was a graveyard of hulks, where James A White carried on a salvage and scrap recovery business, occasionally breaking up navy ships. The Black Swan frigate MODESTE (1,470 tons 1945) is berthed at the outer breakwater probably on 17 March 1961 soon after she arrived from Portsmouth on 11 March. Her net value was £17,458 from 1,017 tons of saleable material.

The Hunt class destroyer TALYBONT (1,087 tons 1943) at Shipbreaking Industries' Charlestown yard on 17 March 1961. She had previously been a static training vessel at Rosyth before being handed over to BISCO and towed the two miles west on 14 February. She still sports a full outfit of depth charge throwers and rails.

TALYBONT at the Charlestown demolition berth with its two 12-ton Scotch derricks on 17 March 1961, which more or less dried out at low tide. The other berths were for lay-by ships, including the outer breakwater with a trawler lying alongside, possibly KINORD. The plate from one of her two boilers shows the usual 300 lb/sq in working pressure of most WW2 destroyers, which from the date was tested after the boiler was shipped post launch.

A close-up of TALYBONT's bridge structure on 17 March 1961. Her armament had been removed by the Admiralty, but not her rangefinder/director. The maker's plate from her near sister WILTON shows that it was made by English Electric, who produced a huge range of equipment during WW2, from generators, steam turbines, electric motors, diesel engines for T class submarines, Comet tanks, Halifax bombers, radar and directors to RPC systems.

The forward end of TALYBONT's engine room after the deck had been removed. No doubt many artificers trained at HMS Caledonia had stood in front of these gauges and controls. Her saleable outturn was 915 tons with a net value of £19,954.

The 'S' class submarine SOLENT (715 tons 1944) at Troon's inner harbour on 26 October 1961. She had arrived on 28 August from lay-up in the Gareloch after service as a battery charging and logistics tender to the high underwater speed trials submarine SCOTSMAN. She was drawing 13ft, but at low tide has heeled to starboard to rest on her starboard external ballast tank. The BP tanker astern is BRITISH PATIENCE.

OCEAN (13,190 tons 1945) was another light fleet carrier to go for scrap after the RN found itself unable to maintain more than three or four carriers in service. She was towed to Faslane by ADVICE, arriving on 6 May 1962. Four weeks later on 4 June, demolition is well under way at No.1 berth.

OCEAN's flight deck looking aft from amidships on 4 June 1962 – though the guardrails show that she had not been engaged on flying operations latterly, having been used for training with classrooms and accommodation built into the hangar, before being laid up at Devonport from 1957.

Much of OCEAN's island has been dismantled by 4 June, although that part displaying her pennant number R68 still remains.

Later on that same day, 4 June, more of OCEAN's island has been removed. The hangar is well revealed, starting to be filled with items for lifting ashore.

OCEAN's flight deck looking forward on 4 June, with her faded deck recognition letter 'O'. Unlike the fleet carriers, her flight deck was not armoured.

OCEAN on 4 June at Shipbreaking Industries' yard on the Gareloch. The distinctive stern shape of the light fleet carriers is revealed, with its riveted shell seam strakes - welding tended to be used on butt joints and internal structure at the time.

This photo seems to have been taken standing in the forward aircraft lift well in the hangar deck, recessed for the lift platform in its lowered position to be flush with the deck, so probably also on 4 June. The forward boiler room is below and behind it, from where OCEAN's boiler test plate came (two in each machinery space). The test is dated 16 months after her completion by Stephen in August 1945. One of her steam turbine rotors needed replacing in December 1945, so perhaps she had further machinery problems.

An almost unrecognisable OCEAN at Faslane on 13 November 1962. She was moved to the beaching ground on 12 December. She yielded 10,348 tons of saleable material and 1,223 tons of rubbish. It took an average of 60 men 44 weeks to demolish her, at an average pay of 5s 4d per hour (£0.27) – the minimum wage today being some 25 times greater.

INDEX